101 Facts About

PREDATORS

101 FACTS ABOUT

POLAR BEARS

Julia Barnes

Gareth Stevens Publishing
A WORLD ALMANAC EDUCATION GROUP COMPANY

Please visit our web site at: www.garethstevens.com
For a free color catalog describing Gareth Stevens Publishing's
list of high-quality books and multimedia programs,
call 1-800-542-2595 (USA) or 1-800-387-3178 (Canada).
Gareth Stevens Publishing's fax: (414) 332-3567.

Library of Congress Cataloging-in-Publication Data

Barnes, Julia, 1955-
    101 facts about polar bears / by Julia Barnes. — North American ed.
      p. cm. — (101 facts about predators)
    Includes bibliographical references and index.
    Summary: Presents information about the physical characteristics, habitat,
and behavior of polar bears.
    ISBN 0-8368-4038-0 (lib. bdg.)
    1. Polar bear—Miscellanea—Juvenile literature. [1. Polar bear—Miscellanea.
2. Bears—Miscellanea.] I. Title: One hundred one facts about polar bears.
II. Title: One hundred and one facts about polar bears. III. Title.
QL737.C27B358   2004
599.786—dc22   2003059176

This North American edition first published in 2004 by
Gareth Stevens Publishing
A World Almanac Education Group Company
330 West Olive Street, Suite 100
Milwaukee, WI 53212 USA

This U.S. edition copyright © 2004 by Gareth Stevens, Inc. Original edition © 2003 by First
Stone Publishing. First published in 2003 by First Stone Publishing, 4/5 The Marina,
Harbour Road, Lydney, Gloucestershire, GL15 5ET, United Kingdom. Additional end
matter © 2004 by Gareth Stevens, Inc.

First Stone Series Editor: Claire Horton-Bussey
First Stone Designer: Sarah Williams
Geographical consultant: Miles Ellison
Gareth Stevens Editor: Catherine Gardner

Printed in Hong Kong through Printworks Int. Ltd.

1 2 3 4 5 6 7 8 9 08 07 06 05 04

WHAT IS A PREDATOR?

Predators are nature's hunters – the creatures that must kill in order to survive. They come in all shapes and sizes, ranging from the mighty tiger to a slithering snake. Although predators are different in many ways, they do have some things in common. All predators are necessary in the balance of nature. Predators keep the number of other animals in control, preventing disease and starvation. In addition, all predators adapted, or changed, to survive where they live. They developed special skills to find prey and kill it in the quickest, simplest way possible.

In the arctic, the polar bear is the top predator. It can hunt on the frozen land and in the icy sea. Its sense of smell helps it find **prey** hidden by snow or ice. It can grab a meal with one swipe of its mighty paw. No arctic animal challenges this big bear.

101 Facts About POLAR BEARS

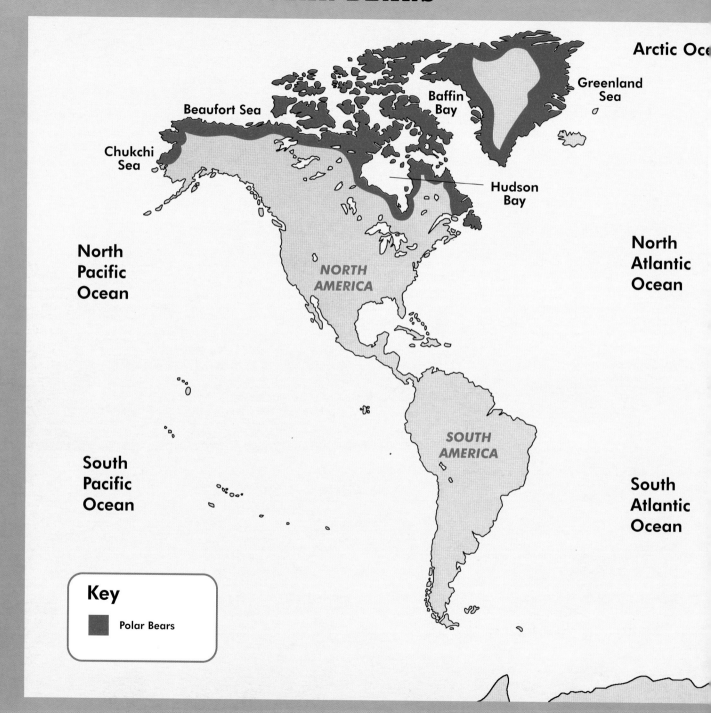

Arctic Oce[an]

Greenland
Sea

Baffin
Bay

Beaufort Sea

Chukchi
Sea

Hudson Bay

North
Pacific
Ocean

North
Atlantic
Ocean

NORTH
AMERICA

South
Pacific
Ocean

SOUTH
AMERICA

South
Atlantic
Ocean

Key

Polar Bears

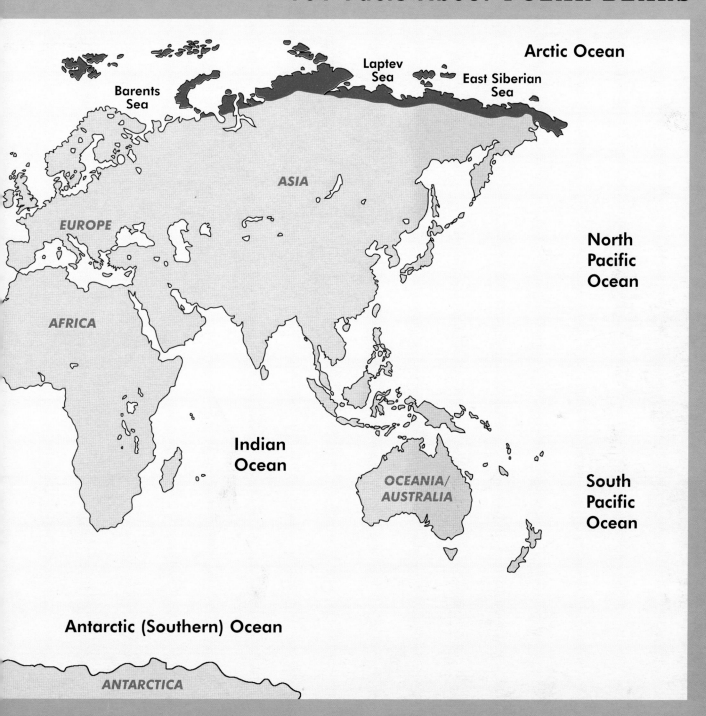

101 Facts About POLAR BEARS

Arctic Ocean

Laptev Sea

East Siberian Sea

Barents Sea

ASIA

EUROPE

North Pacific Ocean

AFRICA

Indian Ocean

OCEANIA/ AUSTRALIA

South Pacific Ocean

Antarctic (Southern) Ocean

ANTARCTICA

1 The polar bear is the biggest four-legged **carnivore** on Earth.

2 The scientific name for the polar bear is *Ursus maritimus,* which means marine, or sea, bear.

3 Scientists have found **fossils** of bears that lived about twenty million years ago. These bears were smaller, stockier, and more doglike than today's bears.

4 Over millions of years, the doglike bears grew bigger. They began to look more like the brown bears (below) that now live in Asia, Europe, and North America.

5 During the Ice Age, the brown bears that lived in Siberia traveled farther north. They were stranded when the **glaciers** retreated.

6 The bears that became stranded in the **polar** areas learned to find food in the sea and to get along in the freezing temperatures.

7 Over time, the bears' features changed. The bears that lived in the arctic became quite different from brown bears. This new type of bear was called a polar bear (right).

8 Polar bears live in one of the coldest places on Earth – the ice-covered waters of the arctic circle. (See pages 4-5.)

9 During the short arctic summers, temperatures reach about 32° Fahrenheit (0° Celsius). In the coldest months of the year, however, temperatures can fall below -90° F (-68° C).

10 In the far north of the arctic, only two land **mammals** survive the cold weather and the frozen ground: the polar bear and the arctic fox (below).

11 The polar bear has huge paws. They act like snowshoes that keep the bear safe on thin ice.

12 Thick fur covers the soles of the polar bear's feet. The fur keeps out the cold and helps the bear walk on the ice.

13 Each foot has five toes armed with curved claws. The claws help the polar bear grip the ice and catch slippery prey.

14 The polar bear's teeth have sharp cutting edges for tearing through meat.

15 Its white fur coat helps camouflage, or hide, the polar bear in its snowy surroundings (above). The arctic ground is covered with snow all year.

16 In fact, polar bears are not pure white.

They are light yellow or cream colored. Their skin under the fur coat is black.

17 A polar bear's coat has two layers: the outer coat, which is 6 inches (15 centimeters) long, and a thick, **waterproof** undercoat with hairs that are 2 inches (5 cm) long.

20 A layer of blubber covers nearly all of a polar bear's body. In some places, the blubber can be 5 inches (12 cm) thick.

18 Its special fur, along with a thick layer of body fat, help keep the polar bear warm (above).

21 At certain times of the year, an adult polar bear has 220 pounds (100 kilograms) of fat, which is about 40 percent of its total body weight.

19 When prey is easy to find, a polar bear eats lots of food. It eats big meals to gain a thick layer of fat, called blubber, under its skin.

22 If food is in very short supply, the polar bear retreats into a den, where it may stay for fifty days or more. It lives off its layer of fat.

23 Polar bears do not **hibernate** in the same way as other animals. The male and young female polar bears roam the ice all winter long.

24 The polar bear has a smaller head, a longer neck, and a more **streamlined** body than the brown bear.

25 The shape of the polar bear's body is ideal for swimming (below). A polar bear is able to swim about 60 to 70 miles (95 to 112 kilometers) or more without landing.

26 In water, the polar bear's front paws become powerful paddles, while the back legs provide balance and steering.

27 A polar bear (below) swims through the water at speeds of 6 miles (10 km) per hour. It can remain underwater for two minutes at a time.

28 Measuring about 8 feet (2.5 meters) from its nose to the tip of its tail, the adult male polar bear ranks as the strongest and biggest of the eight different **species** of bear.

29 Male polar bears weigh between 770 and 1,320 pounds (350 and 600 kg). The females are much lighter. Some females are as light as 330 pounds (150 kg).

30 The polar bear is surprisingly agile for its size (right). It jumps over 6.5-foot (2-m) ice ridges and leaps down 20-foot (6-m) walls of ice.

31 A strong predator, the polar bear can hunt prey that is larger than it is, such as a 1,320-pound (600-kg) beluga whale or a 2,200-pound (1,000-kg) adult walrus.

32 Most often, a polar bear eats one of the many kinds of seals: harp, bearded, ringed, or hooded seals. The bear most needs the animal's blubber and may not eat the rest.

33 If times are hard, the polar bear can make do with seabirds, bird eggs, fish, shellfish, berries, mushrooms, and kelp, which is a type of seaweed.

an average of 4.4 pounds (2 kg) of fat per day, but it does not need to eat every day. It does not cache, or store, meat left from a kill.

34 A polar bear also **scavenges** on the **carcasses** of dead animals (above). Bears that live near human settlements sniff out food in garbage dumps and garbage cans.

35 To survive, the polar bear needs to eat

36 The polar bear is a patient hunter. It finds a hole in the ice and waits — sometimes for an hour or more — until a seal comes to the surface.

37 When a seal comes up through a hole, the polar bear uses its jaws to grab the seal's head or upper body and then flips it onto the ice.

38 In summer, seals leave the ocean water and spend some time on the land. The polar bear must use different hunting skills to find its next meal.

39 A polar bear can smell a seal that is 20 miles (30 km) away. As the bear gets closer, it creeps up on its prey.

40 As the polar bear sneaks within 50 feet (15 m) of its prey, it charges and grabs the seal with its teeth and claws.

41 A charging polar bear can move fast (below), reaching speeds of 25 miles (40 km) per hour for short bursts.

42 At other times, the polar bear prowls underwater, then suddenly surfaces at the edge of the ice to grab a seal.

43 Polar bears prefer to live alone rather than in a group. In summer and autumn, they live on the edge of the pack ice, where they can find plenty of seals to hunt.

44 In winter, when the water freezes, polar bears spread over a wider area. Walking at an average speed of 3 miles (5 km) per hour, a polar bear can cover 20 miles (32 km) or more in a single day.

45 A polar bear is one of the few animals that can walk like a human, with its heel touching the ground before its toes.

46 Polar bears can stand and even walk a few steps on their two hind legs (right). They stand up to get a better view of the land as they search for seals that are resting in the sun.

47 As it looks for prey and follows the freezing and thawing ice, a polar bear travels long distances. Many bears share the same **territory**.

48 Polar bears are not loners all of the time. Sometimes they gather in groups of as many as one hundred (right).

49 A group of polar bears may gather to feed on a large whale carcass. A garbage dump may also attract a big group of polar bears.

50 In Hudson Bay and other areas where the ice melts for the summer, polar bears gather together on land.

51 When polar bears do gather in big groups, they seem to get along well and may even enjoy some friendly wrestling.

52 In April and May, male and female polar bears (above) come together to breed.

53 Male polar bears follow the scent of the females that are ready for breeding for as many as 62 miles (100 km).

54 Females that have young cubs do not breed. Each spring, there are more male polar bears than females that can breed.

55 To win a chance to breed, males fight each other. They often stand upright, hissing and roaring. A fight may end in injury but rarely ends in death.

56 The strongest male chases away the others. He stays with the female for about a week.

57 When a female is **pregnant**, she starts to build up the amount of fat in her body. She must gain about 440 pounds (200 kg) of fat in order to give birth to healthy cubs.

58 A pregnant female builds a special den in October. The den protects her and her cubs in winter.

59 To build a den, the female digs a long tunnel. At the end is at least one chamber, or small room.

60 A layer of snow, as thick as 140 inches (350 cm), protects the den's chamber from blowing snow and icy temperatures.

61 Once the bear curls up inside the den, the temperature stays about 43° F (6° C) higher than the outside temperature.

62 The female (below) stays in her den for the next 100 to 170 days. She gives birth in the den and rests with her new cubs. They live there until March or April.

polar bears have two cubs in a litter. A single cub and triplets are less common.

63 While the pregnant polar bear is in her warm den, she hibernates. Her heart rate slows from its normal resting rate of about 46 beats per minute to about 27 beats per minute.

64 Between November and January, the female gives birth. Usually,

65 Newborn cubs (left) are small and helpless, but they have fine coats of fur. At birth, the cubs weigh about 21 ounces (600 grams).

66 For the first weeks of their lives, young cubs cannot see. They curl up close to their mother to keep warm. They drink her milk, sleep, and grow.

67 A polar bear's milk is very rich, and the cubs grow quickly.

68 By the time the cubs are four weeks old, they can open their eyes. At the age of two months, they have grown teeth and a coat of thick, white fur, and they can walk around the den.

69 When they leave the den in early spring, the cubs (right) need to get used to the cold. Their legs must grow stronger, and they must learn to swim.

70 For a few weeks, the cubs spend most of their time in their den. They leave the safety of the den for short periods of time.

71 Cubs weigh about 22 pounds (10 kg) when they are three or four months old. They still drink their mother's milk.

72 When the cubs make their first trip to the sea ice (below), they pause many times to feed and to rest. It can be a slow trip for the hungry mother bear.

73 The mother bear is patient and caring with her little cubs. She risks her life to attack any animal that might harm her cubs.

74 When they reach the icy sea, the mother polar bear begins to hunt, and the cubs eat solid food for the first time.

75 Once a cub begins to eat solid food, it gains weight quickly. A cub weighs about 100 pounds (45 kg) by the time it turns eight months old.

76 Little cubs learn how to hunt by watching their mother's skills (above). In the first year, the cubs try to catch prey, but often they are not successful.

77 By the time they are two years old, the young bears spend more of their time hunting. They may catch a seal for a meal every five to six days.

78 When the cubs are about thirty months old, they can live alone, and the mother can breed again. If an adult male is near, the mother or the male chases the cubs away.

79 Sometimes, a small group of **subadults** feed and travel together for short periods of time until they are ready to breed.

81 In the wild, a polar bear lives for twenty to twenty-five years. It is the arctic's biggest predator. The only enemies it has to fear are human hunters.

82 The people **native** to northern regions have used polar bear meat and **pelts**. Hunting by these small groups of people did not greatly affect the number of polar bears.

80 Young female bears start to breed when they turn four or five years old. Males are not ready to compete with each other for females until they reach six years of age (above).

83 More people started to explore the arctic and hunt the polar bears in the twentieth century.

84 The earliest hunters needed to eat the polar bear meat. In later years, hunters shot animals for fun, and polar bears were big **trophies**.

85 Hunters often shot the bears from planes. They could catch many more bears from the air.

86 Hunting polar bears from planes is now illegal, and most countries limit the number of bears hunters may kill.

87 Every year, about seven hundred polar bears are killed by human hunters.

88 Human hunters are not the only danger to polar bears. Human neighbors often threaten to take over the land polar bears need.

89 More and more people settle in areas close to polar bears. They set up weather stations, drill for and refine oil, run seal and whale processing plants, and build small towns.

90 Human activity can pollute or destroy the habitat of polar bears and spoil their food supply.

91 Polar bears are alway searching for an easy meal. They often look around cities or towns, where they can raid garbage dumps or grab food left in cars (above).

92 Attacks on humans by polar bears have

been rare, but the number may increase as people and bears have more contact.

with special darts and then flying them farther north by helicopter (below).

93 Churchill, Canada, is called the Polar Bear Capital of the World. Large numbers of polar bears gather there each year in the early months of winter.

94 A Polar Bear Alert Team looks out for bears that come too close to Churchill and moves about one hundred bears a year.

95 Experts move bears by **sedating** them

96 Many people visit Churchill each year to see the large polar bear gathering. Guides take out groups of people who want to see the bears up close in the wild (above).

97 Experts think that 22,000 to 27,000 polar bears live in the wild.

98 Polar bears are not in danger of dying out right now, but they might be in trouble if humans keep moving into the arctic.

99 Growing demands by people for oil, natural gas, and land may push the polar bear out of its arctic home.

100 Scientists think the temperature on Earth is rising slowly over time. They fear the warmer weather will affect the polar bear's habitat and prey.

101 The polar bear is one of the world's most amazing predators. It survives bitterly cold weather and dangerous ice. Can it survive threats from humans?

Glossary

carcasses: bodies of dead animals.

carnivore: a meat-eating animal.

fossils: the remains of animals or plants that can be seen in rocks.

glaciers: huge sheets of ice that can move across land or down slopes.

hibernate: to spend the winter in a deep sleep in which all the body functions are slowed down.

mammals: warm-blooded animals that feed their young milk from the mother's body.

native: the first people who live in a certain place.

pelts: skins and furs of animals.

polar: around Earth's North and South Poles.

predators: animals that kill other animals for food.

pregnant: having babies growing inside a female's body.

prey: the animal that a predator chooses to hunt and kill.

scavenges: feeds on the body of a dead animal.

sedating: putting to sleep for a short period with special drugs.

species: a type of animal or plant.

streamlined: shaped to glide easily through water.

subadults: young animals that have left their mothers but are still too young to breed.

territory: an area of land that an animal claims as its own.

trophies: animals that are killed for sport and displayed.

waterproof: able to keep water out.

More Books to Read

Great Ice Bear: The Polar Bear and the Eskimo
Dorothy Hinshaw Patent
(William Morrow)

Polar Bears
Emilie U. Lepthien
(Children's Press)

Polar Bears (Creatures in White)
Wendy Pfeffer
(Silver Burdett)

Polar Bears (Our Wild World Series)
Linda Tagliaferro
(Creative Publishing)

Web Sites

Bering Land Bridge Preserve
www.nps.gov/bela/html/polar.htm

Polar Bear Education
www.seaworld.org/infobooks/
PolarBears/home.html

Polar Bears International
www.polarbearsalive.org/facts2.php

Polar World
www.polarworld.com

To find additional web sites, use a reliable search engine to find one or more of the following keywords: **arctic circle**, **harp seal**, **polar bear.**

 # Index